TO BE A SUCCESSFUL

FOREX TRADER

Ultimate step by step how to become a successful Forex trader

JAMES C. MORISSON

This book is a work of nonfiction. While every effort has been made to ensure the accuracy of the information provided and to present it in a comprehensive and unbiased manner

TABLE OF CONTENT

INTRODUCTION

In a small town, Benjamin discovered a book on forex trading. He immersed himself in its pages, learning strategies and techniques. With practice, he became skilled at reading the markets. Benjamin's talent was noticed by an investment firm, and he joined as a forex analyst. His success grew, and he became a respected figure in the industry, inspiring others with his story. Benjamin's journey showed the power of knowledge and perseverance, encouraging others to chase their dreams.

Forex Trading: An Introduction to the Global Currency Market
Forex trading is the buying and selling of currencies in the foreign exchange market.

It's the largest and most liquid financial market worldwide, with daily trading volumes surpassing $6 trillion. Participants include banks, corporations, and retail traders.
Currency pairs, such as EUR/USD, represent the exchange rate between two currencies. Exchange rates fluctuate due to economic factors and market sentiment. Leverage allows traders to control larger positions with less capital, but it also amplifies risks. Traders use technical analysis (chart patterns, indicators) and fundamental analysis (economic indicators, policies) to make informed decisions.

Risk management is crucial in mitigating potential losses.Forex trading presents opportunities for profit, but it carries inherent risks. Understanding the market and employing effective strategies are key to success in this dynamic and exciting financial realm.

Chapter 1: Understanding the Forex Market

The largest and most liquid financial market in the world is the Forex market, sometimes referred to as the foreign exchange market.. It operates 24 hours a day, five days a week, and facilitates the trading of currencies from various countries. Understanding the Forex market is essential for anyone interested in global finance, trading, or investing. In this comprehensive guide, we will delve into the fundamental concepts, participants, major currency pairs, and key factors that influence the Forex market.

1. What is the Forex Market?
The Forex market is a decentralized market where currencies are bought and sold. It functions through a network of global financial institutions, such as banks, central banks, hedge funds, corporations, and individual traders. Unlike traditional stock markets, Forex trading doesn't take place on a centralized exchange. Instead, it operates through an electronic network of participants.

2. Currency Pairs:
Forex trading involves the simultaneous buying of one currency and selling another. Currencies are always quoted in pairs, such as EUR/USD,

GBP/USD, or USD/JPY.The base currency is the first currency in the pair, while the quote currency is the second currency. Understanding currency pairs is crucial, as the exchange rate between them determines the value of one currency relative to another.

3. Market Participants:
The Forex market is composed of various participants, each with unique roles. These participants include central banks, commercial banks, institutional investors, retail traders, multinational corporations, and speculators. Central banks play a significant role by implementing monetary policies and intervening in the Forex market to stabilize their domestic currencies.

4. There are three main trading sessions on the Forex market: the Asian session, the European session, and the American session. Each session has its own characteristics and trading volume. However, the Forex market operates 24 hours a day due to the overlap of these sessions. This constant availability provides traders with ample opportunities to participate in the market at their convenience.

5. Factors Influencing Forex Market:
Several factors impact the Forex market and drive currency fluctuations. These include economic indicators (GDP, inflation, employment data), central bank policies (interest rates, monetary

easing or tightening), geopolitical events (wars, elections, trade disputes), and market sentiment (investor confidence and risk appetite). Understanding these factors and their potential impact on currency prices is crucial for successful Forex trading.

6. Fundamental and Technical Analysis:
Traders employ various strategies to analyze the Forex market. Fundamental analysis involves evaluating economic data, geopolitical events, and central bank policies to predict currency movements. Technical analysis, on the other hand, focuses on chart patterns, indicators, and historical price data to identify trends and potential trading opportunities. A combination of both approaches can provide a comprehensive view of the market.

7. Risk Management:
Forex trading carries inherent risks, and it is essential to implement sound risk management strategies. Traders often utilize techniques such as setting stop-loss orders, diversifying their portfolio, and managing position sizes to limit potential losses. Understanding and managing risk is crucial to preserving capital and long-term success in the Forex market.

Conclusion:
Understanding the Forex market is a valuable skill for anyone interested in global finance and trading. This comprehensive guide has provided an

overview of the Forex market, including its structure, participants, major currency pairs, and key factors that influence currency movements. By grasping these concepts and employing proper risk management techniques, individuals can navigate the Forex market with confidence and potentially achieve their financial goals. Remember, continuous learning and staying updated with market developments are crucial for success in this dynamic and ever-

Chapter 2: Developing a Solid Trading Foundation

Financial market trading may be a thrilling and financially rewarding endeavor. However, it is important to approach trading with a solid foundation to increase your chances of success. A strong trading foundation involves acquiring the necessary knowledge, developing key skills, and adopting the right mindset. In this article, we will explore the essential elements of building a solid trading foundation.

1. Education and Research:
To develop a solid trading foundation, it is crucial to educate yourself about the financial markets and trading principles. Start by understanding the basics of trading, such as different asset classes (stocks, bonds, commodities, forex, etc.), market dynamics, and various trading strategies. You can explore a wide range of educational resources, including books, online courses, webinars, and seminars. Take the time to research and stay updated on market news, economic indicators, and company-specific information. Continuous learning and staying informed are key aspects of building a strong foundation in trading.

2. Understanding Risk Management:
Successful traders understand the importance of risk management. Risk management involves assessing and controlling the potential risks associated with trading. This includes determining an acceptable level of risk for each trade, setting stop-loss orders to limit potential losses, and using proper position sizing techniques. By managing risk effectively, you protect your trading capital and avoid significant losses, which is crucial for long-term success.

3. Developing a Trading Plan:
A well-defined trading plan is essential for consistent and disciplined trading. A trading plan outlines your trading goals, strategies, entry and exit criteria, risk management rules, and other relevant parameters. It helps you make objective decisions based on predetermined rules rather than it succumbing to emotions or impulsive actions. Regularly review and update your trading plan as market conditions and your trading experience evolve.

4. Practicing on a Demo Account:
Before risking real money, it is highly recommended to practice trading on a demo account. Most brokerage platforms offer demo accounts that simulate real-market conditions without involving actual funds. This allows you to test your trading strategies, refine your skills, and

gain experience in a risk-free environment. Use the demo account to understand the mechanics of trading, familiarize yourself with the trading platform, and develop your confidence before transitioning to live trading.

5. Embracing Discipline and Emotional Control:
Trading requires discipline and emotional control. It is common for traders to experience various emotions such as fear, greed, or impatience, which can lead to poor decision-making. To build a solid foundation, you must learn to detach emotions from your trading decisions and stick to your predetermined trading plan. Implementing strict discipline in following your rules and avoiding impulsive actions is essential for long-term success in trading.

6. Building a Support Network:
Trading can be a solitary activity, but it is beneficial to build a support network of like-minded individuals. Engage with other traders, either through online communities, forums, or local trading groups. Share ideas, experiences, and challenges with fellow traders to gain insights and different perspectives. Additionally, consider finding a mentor or joining a trading education program to accelerate your learning and receive guidance from experienced professionals.

7. Continuous Evaluation and Adaptation:

The financial markets are dynamic and ever-changing, requiring traders to continuously evaluate and adapt their strategies. Regularly assess your trading performance, identify areas for improvement, and make necessary adjustments. Keep a trading journal to record your trades, analyze your successes and failures, and learn from them. This process of self-evaluation and adaptation is vital for growth and long-term success in trading.

In conclusion, developing a solid trading foundation is a critical step towards becoming a successful trader. By investing time in education, understanding risk management, developing a trading plan, practicing on a demo account, embracing discipline, building a support network, and continuously evaluating and adapting your strategies,

Chapter 3: Fundamental Analysis

Fundamental analysis is a technique for determining an asset's intrinsic value, such as the value of a stock, bond, or commodity. It involves examining various factors that can influence the value of the asset, including economic indicators, financial statements, industry trends, and company-specific data. By assessing these fundamental factors, investors aim to determine whether an asset is overvalued, undervalued, or fairly priced, helping them make informed investment decisions.

The core idea behind fundamental analysis is that the true value of an asset is determined by its underlying fundamentals. These fundamentals include both qualitative and quantitative factors. Qualitative factors encompass aspects such as the company's management team, competitive advantage, brand reputation, and industry positioning. Quantitative factors, on the other hand, involve analyzing financial statements, ratios, earnings, cash flows, and other numerical data.

One of the primary sources of information for fundamental analysis is the company's financial statements, which include the balance sheet, income statement, and cash flow statement. These documents provide a snapshot of a company's financial health, including its assets, liabilities, revenues, expenses, and cash flows. By analyzing these statements, investors can assess factors such as profitability, liquidity, solvency, and overall financial stability.

In addition to financial statements, fundamental analysis considers macroeconomic factors and industry trends. Economic indicators, such as GDP growth rates, inflation rates, and employment figures, can provide insights into the overall health of the economy. Industry trends, such as technological advancements, regulatory changes, and market demand, can influence the prospects of a specific company or sector. By examining these factors, investors can gain a broader understanding of the potential opportunities and risks associated with an investment.

Fundamental analysis also involves comparing the financial performance of a company with its competitors and industry peers. This comparative analysis helps investors assess a company's competitive position, market share, and growth prospects. Additionally, fundamental analysis looks at qualitative factors like corporate governance, management expertise, and strategic initiatives. These factors can have a significant impact on a company's long-term prospects and value.

It is important to note that fundamental analysis is just one approach to evaluating investments. Other methods, such as technical analysis, focus on price patterns and market trends. While fundamental analysis provides a more comprehensive view of an investment's value, it does not guarantee future performance. Market dynamics, investor sentiment, and unforeseen events can all influence the price of an asset, regardless of its underlying fundamentals.

In conclusion, fundamental analysis is a critical tool used by investors to assess the intrinsic value of financial assets. By examining a combination of qualitative and quantitative factors, investors aim to make informed investment decisions. While fundamental analysis provides valuable insights, it should be complemented with other forms of analysis and considered alongside market conditions and investor sentiment.

Chapter 4: Technical Analysis

Technical analysis is a methodology used in financial markets to forecast future price movements by analyzing historical market data. It is based on the belief that historical price patterns, trading volume, and other market data can provide insights into the future direction of prices. Technical analysis is commonly used in various financial markets, including stocks, commodities, currencies, and cryptocurrencies.

The core principle of technical analysis is that market prices follow trends and patterns that can be identified and analyzed to make informed trading decisions. Traders who employ technical analysis, known as technical analysts, use various tools and techniques to study price charts and other market data.

One of the fundamental concepts in technical analysis is the notion of support and resistance levels. Support levels are price levels where demand for an asset is expected to be strong enough to prevent prices from falling further. Resistance levels, on the other hand, are price levels where selling pressure is expected to be strong enough to prevent prices from rising further. Technical analysts look for these levels on price charts and consider them important reference points for determining entry and exit points for trades.

Another widely used tool in technical analysis is trend analysis. Technical analysts examine price charts to identify trends in the market, which can be classified as upward (bullish), downward (bearish), or sideways (consolidation). Trend lines are drawn on price charts to visually represent the direction and strength of a trend. Traders often look for opportunities to buy or sell assets when a trend is confirmed, believing that prices are more likely to continue moving in the direction of the trend.

Indicators are also an integral part of technical analysis. These are mathematical calculations based on historical price data that provide additional information about the market.Leading indicators and trailing indicators are two sorts of indicators. Leading indicators attempt to provide signals in advance of future price movements, while lagging indicators follow price movements and provide confirmation or validation of the trend. Some commonly used indicators include moving averages, oscillators (such as the relative strength index and stochastic oscillator), and volume-based indicators.

Technical analysts also pay attention to chart patterns, which are formed by price movements over time. These patterns can provide insights into the psychology of market participants and can indicate potential future price movements. Some well-known chart patterns include head and shoulders, double tops and bottoms, triangles, and flags. Traders who specialize in chart pattern analysis aim to identify these patterns as they emerge and take advantage of the anticipated price movements.

It is important to note that technical analysis is not without its limitations. Critics argue that it relies heavily on historical data and patterns, which may not always accurately predict future price movements. Furthermore, technical analysis does not take Into account fundamental factors such as economic indicators, company financials, and news events that can significantly impact market prices.

Despite these criticisms, technical analysis remains a popular and widely used approach in financial markets. Many traders and investors find value in studying price charts and using technical tools to make informed trading decisions. It is often used in conjunction with other forms of analysis, such as fundamental analysis, to gain a more comprehensive view of the market.

In conclusion, technical analysis is a methodology used to forecast future price movements by analyzing historical market data. It employs tools and techniques such as support and resistance levels, trend analysis, indicators, and chart patterns to identify potential trading opportunities. While technical analysis has its limitations, it continues to be an essential tool for many traders and investors in their pursuit of profitable trades.

Chapter 5: Developing Effective Trading Strategies

Trading in financial markets can be a lucrative endeavor, but it also carries risks. To navigate the complexities of the market and increase the chances of success, traders need to develop effective trading strategies. These strategies are a set of rules and guidelines that help traders make informed decisions about when to enter or exit trades, manage risk, and maximize profitability. In this article, we will explore some key elements of developing effective trading strategies.

1. Define Your Trading Goals: The first step in developing a trading strategy is to clearly define your goals.Are you seeking long-term investments or quick profits? Are swing trading or day trading more appealing to you? Knowing your goals will enable you to adjust your plan as necessary.

2. Conduct Market Analysis: Before executing any trade, it is crucial to conduct thorough market analysis. This includes analyzing various factors such as market trends, economic indicators, news events, and technical analysis indicators. By understanding the market conditions, you can identify potential trading opportunities and make more informed decisions.

3. Choose Your Trading Style: There are different trading styles, each with its own set of strategies. Some popular trading styles include trend following, breakout trading, mean reversion, and momentum trading. is crucial to pick a trading approach that fits your temperament, level of risk tolerance, and time commitment.

4. Develop Entry and Exit Rules: One of the critical components of a trading strategy is defining clear entry and exit rules. Entry rules determine when to enter a trade, while exit rules specify when to exit a trade to lock in profits or limit losses. These rules can be based on technical indicators, price patterns, or a combination of both. It is essential to backtest your entry and exit rules using historical data to evaluate their effectiveness.

5.Implement Risk Management: Risk management is a vital aspect of any trading strategy. It involves determining the maximum amount of capital you are willing to risk on each trade and setting stop-loss orders to limit potential losses. By managing risk effectively, you protect your trading capital and avoid large drawdowns that can be difficult to recover from.

6. Monitor and Adapt: Markets are dynamic, and trading strategies need to adapt accordingly. Regularly monitor your trades and the overall performance of your strategy. If you notice consistent patterns of success or failure, consider adjusting your strategy to capitalize on strengths and address weaknesses.

7. Emotions and Discipline: Emotions can often cloud judgment and lead to impulsive trading decisions. Developing discipline is crucial in sticking to your trading strategy and avoiding emotional trading. Maintain a trading journal to track your trades and emotions, which can help you identify patterns and improve your decision-making process.

8. Continual Learning: The world of trading is ever-evolving, and there is always something new to learn. Stay updated with market news, economic events, and industry trends. Continually educate yourself about trading strategies, technical analysis, and risk management techniques. Engage in discussions with other traders and participate in educational programs to enhance your trading skills.

In conclusion, developing effective trading strategies requires careful planning, analysis, and risk management. By defining your goals, conducting market analysis, choosing a trading style, and implementing sound risk management techniques, you can increase your chances of success in the financial markets. Remember to stay disciplined, adapt to market conditions, and continually educate yourself to stay ahead in this competitive field.

Chapter 6: Psychology and Emotional Control

Understanding and Managing Your Feelings

Emotions are an inherent part of being human. They color our experiences, shape our relationships, and influence our behavior. However, it's not uncommon for individuals to struggle with emotional control, finding themselves overwhelmed by their feelings or unable to manage them effectively. This is where the field of psychology offers valuable insights and techniques for understanding and mastering emotional control.

Psychology, the scientific study of the mind and behavior, provides us with a framework to explore the complexities of human emotions. It encompasses various theories and approaches that shed light on why we experience emotions and how they impact our lives. Let's delve into some key aspects of psychology that can help us better understand and manage our emotions.

1. Emotional Intelligence:
Emotional intelligence refers to the ability to recognize, understand, and manage our own emotions, as well as recognize and empathize with the emotions of others. It involves being aware of our emotional states, recognizing patterns in our emotional responses, and effectively regulating our

emotions in different situations. Developing emotional intelligence can help us cultivate healthier relationships, make better decisions, and cope with stress more effectively.

2. Cognitive-Behavioral Therapy (CBT):

CBT is a widely-used therapeutic approach in psychology that focuses on identifying and changing negative thought patterns and behaviors. It recognizes that our thoughts and interpretations of events significantly influence our emotions. By challenging and replacing unhelpful thoughts with more realistic and positive ones, individuals can gain better control over their emotional reactions. CBT techniques can be helpful in managing anxiety, depression, anger, and other emotional challenges.

3. Mindfulness:

Mindfulness is a practice derived from ancient contemplative traditions that has gained significant attention in psychology. It involves intentionally paying attention to the present moment, without judgment. By cultivating mindfulness, individuals can become more aware of their emotions as they arise, without getting carried away by them. Mindfulness-based interventions have shown promising results in enhancing emotional regulation, reducing stress, and improving overall well-being.

4. Self-Reflection and Self-Care:

Engaging in self-reflection allows us to gain insight into the root causes of our emotional reactions. By exploring our past experiences, beliefs, and values, we can identify triggers and patterns that contribute to emotional challenges. Self-reflection helps us build self-awareness and develop strategies to respond to emotions in a more balanced and constructive manner. Additionally, practicing self-care, such as getting enough rest, engaging in activities we enjoy, and maintaining healthy relationships, is vital for emotional well-being.

5. Because we are social creatures at our core, our relationships have a big impact on how we feel emotionally. Building and nurturing a support network can provide us with a sense of belonging, understanding, and validation. Talking to trusted friends, family members, or professionals about our emotions can offer new perspectives, guidance, and emotional support. Social support can also help us gain a fresh outlook on challenging situations and find healthy ways to regulate our emotions.

It's important to note that emotional control doesn't mean suppressing or denying emotions but rather understanding and managing them effectively. Psychology offers valuable tools and techniques to navigate the complex terrain of our emotional landscape. By cultivating emotional intelligence, utilizing therapeutic approaches like CBT, practicing mindfulness, engaging in self-reflection,

and seeking social support, individuals can develop greater emotional control and lead more fulfilling lives. Remember, emotional control is a lifelong journey that requires patience, self-compassion, and consistent effort, but the rewards are worth it.
Chapter 7: Money Management and Trade Execution

Chapter 8: Advanced Trading Tools and Techniques

Empowering Traders in the Modern Market

In today's fast-paced and highly competitive financial markets, traders are constantly seeking an edge to enhance their profitability and make informed decisions. To meet this demand, advanced trading tools and techniques have emerged, providing traders with unprecedented insights, analysis, and automation. These tools have revolutionized the trading landscape, empowering both retail and institutional traders to navigate the complexities of the market more efficiently. In this article, we will explore some of the most prominent advanced trading tools and techniques available today and how they can enhance trading strategies.

1. Algorithmic Trading:

Algorithmic trading, commonly referred to as automated trading or algo trading, entails using computer programs to carry out trades in accordance with predetermined guidelines and tactics. Algorithmic trading has gained popularity due to its ability to execute trades with precision, efficiency, and speed, enabling traders to capitalize on even the smallest market inefficiencies.

2. Artificial Intelligence and Machine Learning:

Artificial Intelligence (AI) and Machine Learning (ML) technologies have significantly transformed the trading landscape. By leveraging AI and ML algorithms, traders can analyze massive volumes of historical and real-time data to uncover patterns, predict market movements, and generate actionable insights. These tools can help traders in areas such as sentiment analysis, trend identification, risk assessment, and trade optimization. AI-powered trading platforms can adapt and learn from market data, continuously improving their accuracy and effectiveness.

3. High-Frequency Trading:

High-Frequency Trading (HFT) is a trading strategy that employs powerful computers and sophisticated algorithms to execute a large number of trades within milliseconds. HFT capitalizes on small price discrepancies and market inefficiencies, profiting from rapid execution and high trading volumes. Traders utilizing HFT techniques often have access to co-location services near exchange servers to minimize latency. While HFT has faced scrutiny and regulation due to concerns about market stability and fairness, it remains a prevalent technique in modern trading.

4. Data Analytics and Visualization:

The availability of vast amounts of financial data has made data analytics and visualization tools indispensable for traders. These tools allow traders to analyze historical and real-time market data, identify trends, correlations, and patterns, and make data-driven decisions. Visualization tools present complex data in intuitive and visually appealing ways, enabling traders to identify opportunities and make informed choices with ease. Advanced data analytics techniques, such as predictive analytics and data mining, provide traders with valuable insights into market behavior and can support the development of profitable trading strategies.

5. Risk Management Tools:
Effective risk management is crucial for successful trading. Advanced risk management tools assist traders in identifying, assessing, and mitigating risks associated with their trading activities. These tools utilize techniques such as scenario analysis, stress testing, and value-at-risk (VaR) calculations to quantify and manage risk exposure. Additionally, automated stop-loss orders and position sizing tools can help traders limit losses and control risk in volatile market conditions.

Conclusion:
Advanced trading tools and techniques have transformed the way traders operate in modern financial markets. Algorithmic trading, AI and ML, high-frequency trading, data analytics, and risk management tools have become essential components of traders' arsenals. These tools empower traders to make more informed decisions,

capitalize on market opportunities, and manage risks effectively. As technology continues to advance, traders will have access to even more powerful and sophisticated tools, further enhancing their ability to navigate the complexities of the financial markets.

Chapter 9: Reviewing and Analyzing Trades

Unveiling the Secrets to Successful Investing
Trading in financial markets is an art that requires a combination of knowledge, strategy, and analysis. Whether you are a seasoned investor or a beginner, reviewing and analyzing trades is a crucial step in understanding your performance, identifying strengths and weaknesses, and making informed decisions for future investments. In this article, we will explore the importance of reviewing and analyzing trades and discuss some key strategies to enhance your trading skills.

Why Reviewing and Analyzing Trades Matters:
1. Performance Evaluation: Reviewing and analyzing trades allows you to assess your overall performance as a trader. By scrutinizing past trades, you can identify patterns, measure success rates, and evaluate the effectiveness of your strategies. This evaluation helps you understand what is working and what needs improvement, leading to more informed decision-making in future trades.

2. Learning from Mistakes: Mistakes are an integral part of the learning process in trading. Analyzing trades enables you to identify and learn from your errors, allowing you to avoid repeating them. By pinpointing the reasons behind unsuccessful

trades, you can adjust your strategies and minimize potential losses, ultimately increasing your chances of profitability.

3. Strategy Refinement: Successful trading relies on a well-defined strategy. Reviewing and analyzing trades provides insights into the effectiveness of your current approach. It allows you to fine-tune your strategies based on real-world data, adapting to changing market conditions, and maximizing your potential for success.

Key Strategies for Reviewing and Analyzing Trades:
1. Maintain Detailed Records: Keeping accurate records of your trades is vital for effective analysis. Include information such as entry and exit points, trade duration, market conditions, and reasoning behind each trade. This documentation serves as a valuable resource when reviewing your performance and identifying trends.

2. Utilize Performance Metrics: Implementing performance metrics helps you measure the success of your trades objectively. Key metrics include win-to-loss ratio, average profit/loss per trade, maximum drawdown, and overall return on investment (ROI). Regularly monitoring these metrics helps you identify areas of improvement and set achievable goals.

3. Identify Patterns and Trends: Analyzing trade data helps you identify recurring patterns and trends. By studying historical price movements, candlestick patterns, and technical indicators, you can develop a deeper understanding of market behavior. This knowledge can inform your future trading decisions and enhance your ability to identify potential opportunities.

4. Use Technology and Tools: Take advantage of trading platforms, charting software, and analytical tools to aid in your trade analysis. These resources provide valuable insights, such as historical data, visual representations of price movements, and technical indicators. Utilizing these tools can help you spot trends, execute trades with precision, and make more informed decisions.

5. Seek Expert Opinions and Mentorship: Engaging with experienced traders, joining trading communities, or seeking mentorship from professionals can provide valuable perspectives and insights. Networking with other traders allows you to learn from their experiences and gain new insights into trade analysis. This can help you refine your strategies and stay updated with the latest market trends.

Conclusion:
Reviewing and analyzing trades is an essential aspect of successful trading. By evaluating your performance, learning from mistakes, refining

strategies, and utilizing key strategies, you can enhance your trading skills and increase your chances of profitability. Remember, trade analysis is an ongoing process that requires continuous learning, adaptation, and improvement. With dedication and a systematic approach, you can unlock the secrets to successful investing.

Conclusion

In conclusion, the forex book provides a comprehensive and valuable resource for individuals interested in learning about forex trading. It covers essential topics such as market analysis, technical and fundamental analysis, risk management, and trading strategies. The book equips readers with the necessary knowledge and skills to navigate the complex world of forex trading. By applying the insights and techniques shared in the book, readers can enhance their understanding, make informed trading decisions, and potentially increase their chances of success in the forex market.

FOREX TIME TABLE

www.ingramcontent.com/pod-product-compliance
Lightning Source LLC
Chambersburg PA
CBHW072237230526
45466CB00024B/2101